FOCUS

Teacher's Support Pack

Year 7/8 Number

Lead-in

Elizabeth Kirby   Kathy Pratt

Stanley Thornes (Publishers) Ltd.

developed at the Institute of Education,
University of London

**FOCUS TEACHER'S SUPPORT PACK
NUMBER – LEAD-IN**
Authors: Kathy Pratt and Elizabeth Kirby
Illustrator: Angela Lumley

Text © Kathy Pratt and Elizabeth Kirby
1991
Original illustrations © Stanley Thornes
(Publishers) Ltd 1991

ACKNOWLEDGEMENTS

Professor Celia Hoyles and Dr Richard Noss,
consultants during the development of
Century Maths.

**British Library Cataloguing in
Publication Data**

Century maths: Teacher's support pack:
number – lead-in. – (Century maths)
  I. Series
  510.71

ISBN 0 – 7487 – 1132 – 5

First published in 1991 by
Stanley Thornes (Publishers) Ltd
Old Station Drive, Leckhampton,
Cheltenham GL53 0DN England

Typeset in Melior and Mixage by
Action Typesetting Ltd, Gloucester
Cover design: Chris Gilbert and
Susie Home
Printed and bound by Martin's of Berwick

Contents

Using the Teacher's Support Packs

Each *Teacher's Support Pack* contains:

- help and information relating to the particular Theme or Focus book;
- guidance on problem solving in the classroom;
- further ideas for problem-solving activities;
- direct links with the National Curriculum Attainment Targets;
- detailed computing support;
- advice on cross-curricular links – both with other subject areas and with the National Curriculum Council's cross-curricular themes.

The *Teacher's Support Packs* include a series of double-page spreads – normally one for each section in the Theme material and one for each unit in the Focus texts. These provide an easy source of reference on your desk.

Theme double-page spreads

Each spread includes:

- Main activities
- Materials required
- Computing references
- Teaching suggestions

- Possible links with National Curriculum Attainment Targets
- Detailed references to Focus texts
- Cross-curricular links.

A 'Summary of sections' page sets out the information above in tabular form. It also indicates the scope for mathematical development in each section.

Focus double-page spreads

Focus double-page spreads are similar to those for the Theme books. Most units in a Focus book have a single related double-page spread in the *Teacher's Support Pack*. The main addition in the Focus spreads is a section of Answers to all numbered questions in the pupils' texts.

Materials required

Any special equipment and materials required are listed on the spreads, with the standard icons used in the pupils' texts to show whether they are essential or merely helpful if they are available. (Equipment and materials listed do not include the standard 'basket' of equipment it is assumed will be available in classrooms at all times – see page 16 of each *Teacher's Support Pack*.)

Computing references

Computing activities are integral to Century Maths. There are two main aspects to the use of the computer:

1 *The use of Logo*

Century Maths LogoPack 1 is a package of photocopiable activities designed for use by pupils of all abilities. *Logo 2000* provides materials, including software, which make Logo the natural working environment for many of the mathematical problems which teachers and pupils will want to solve. References to both sets of materials appear throughout the pupil texts.

2 *Other software packages*

References to other software packages are also included in the pupils' materials.

The Logo materials are fully referenced in the double-page spreads for both Theme and Focus material. Some references to other software packages are also included.

Teaching Suggestions

These form the main section in the double-page spreads. They include a general description of the kind of activity to expect. In the Theme spreads they often have a note on the general approach followed by:

- Starting off
- Main activities
- More ideas (when appropriate) and sometimes
- Further activities.

The 'Starting off' section often gives ideas for initial group discussion and ways of organising the groups. The 'More ideas' section may provide comments on extension ideas suggested in the More ideas activities. Related activities are sometimes listed under the 'Further activities' heading.

In the Focus double-page spreads, after a note on the general approach, teaching suggestions are most often set out under unit by unit headings.

Links between Theme and Focus books

The links between Theme and Focus books are set out in the Theme double-page spreads. These Detailed Focus references provide a useful basis for

- planning the follow-up work if you start with a Theme, or
- preparation if you choose to start with the Focus material.

The Focus references indicate the units in the Lead-in (LI), Core (C) and Extension (E) Focus books where related material can be found. These references could be to material which

- would be helpful in working through a Theme;
- would develop skill in the mathematics learned;
- sets the mathematics in another context, enabling the pupil to identify and abstract the mathematics;
- gives further developments which would be of interest to the pupils.

Cross-curricular work

In the Theme *Teacher's Support Packs*, possible links with other subject areas are highlighted, either through links with Attainment Targets or Programmes of Study. These areas are:

- History
- English
- Science
- Geography
- Technology
- NCC cross-curricular themes.

The cross-curricular summary pages offer support and ideas for relevant and constructive cross-curricular work for each Theme.

Problem-solving, record-keeping and assessment

Within the introductory pages you will find a guide to problem solving in the classroom, as well as support and ideas for record-keeping and assessment. (Photocopy masters for record-keeping are provided in the *Worksheet Pack*.)

The range of information and support in the *Teacher's Support Packs* means that they form an integral part of Century Maths for both you and your pupils. They should not be seen merely as answer books or be doomed to collect dust on an inaccessible shelf. They are working documents and are essential support for the pupil materials.

Problem-solving

Why a rationale for problem solving?

Pupils need to experience the application of mathematics in a number of contexts. Opportunities to use mathematical processes should arise from situations meaningful to the learner. Such situations give rise to a number of problems which need to be resolved if a satisfactory solution is to found. However, often the mathematics to be used is not apparent and a great deal of seemingly unnecessary experimentation is undertaken before a solution is reached. The problems encountered may not directly mirror situations met in school but could have common threads of approach. It is the identification of these common threads that enables a pupil to solve a problem.

If pupils are to develop mathematical ability as they grow older, independent thinking needs to be encouraged. This will enable pupils to consider processes by which a problem, or series of problems, can be resolved. These processes may be considered as a series of general strategies that anyone may use in the resolution of a problem. If it is accepted that problem-solving is at the heart of all mathematics, the development of these strategies is crucial for effective mathematical learning.

Some possible general strategies

The notes below relate the strategies to processes involved in developing any Century Maths Theme.

To start with, pupils should be encouraged to *investigate their own problems*. Pupils can be prompted to explore a number of situations and generate their own problems. Mathematical explorations are of value if they do not give rise to the learning of new concepts. Within the context of the chosen situation, ask pupils to:

- list features within the situation that may be considered;

  (Within Century Maths, the 'situation' could be a main activity within a Theme. Discussion with pupils is intended to highlight the features of this activity. From these discussions, pupils could list ideas on which agreement is reached.)

- list the aspects that *can* be changed and those that *cannot* be changed;
- list the mathematical concepts that may be needed;

  (These points should arise from the group discussions, possibly requiring some teacher guidance from an early stage.)

- try to establish what new concepts – if any – are required;

  (This aspect should evolve naturally from the selected Century Maths Theme through statements such as 'We don't know how to do this . . .' and 'We're stuck!')

- ask 'What would happen if . . .?'

  (This stage occurs when pupil confidence has been established in handling problems observed within any particular Century Maths Theme.)

Getting started

Most situations selected by pupils (and anyone else for that matter!) tend to be rather complicated. Talking through the situation allows a variety of thoughts and ideas to be expressed. This will prompt a variety of questions. These will then become the problems to resolve.

Simplifying the situation

At this stage, it is helpful to try to *simplify the situation* through a series of strategies such as:

- specialising – what will happen in a particular case?

- considering reducing
  - the size of the variables (take the simplest case), or
  - the number of variables in use at any one time;
- modelling – making a few assumptions that help to start resolving the problem;
- organising the approach to be taken – random trial and improvement may lead to blind alleys. To avoid these, consider
  - trial and improvement methods;
  - systematic listing of all possiblities;
  - dealing with one variable at a time while holding the others constant.

(Note, however, that blind alleys can often prove to be a rich vein for extending mathematical knowledge even though they may not advance the solution to the problem in hand.)

Representing and recording information

Most people – and that includes pupils – find great difficulty in expressing themselves succinctly when using words and numbers. However, the key to a sound resolution of any situation is the ability to *represent and record information* in such a way that it can be clearly understood and be or benefit to anyone requiring it. To this end, a good diagram or notation is often the key to the successful solution of a problem. Methods of recording information will include:

- informal diagrams and notation;
- pictures and diagrams used to *describe* things clearly;
- tables, graphs, etc. used to *reveal any relationships* within information;
- tables, tree diagrams, matrices, etc. used to *classify* information.

The emphasis should be on *when* to use such representations rather than *how* to use them.

Conjectures and generalisations

At some stage, pupils will start saying they have 'found things out'. This elementary statement is the beginning of their *making and testing conjectures and generalisations*. Within this stage, pupils will have to consider a number of processes, including:

- spotting patterns and relationships of different kinds;
- checking and testing them on further cases;
- trying to find reasons for them;
- making generalisations from particular cases;
- trying to verify the generalisation for all cases;
- moving from number into algebra;
- extending the notation.

Passing through these stages, pupils may feel confident that they have resolved a certain situation and have a sound argument to present. But the most important stage within the problem-solving process is yet to come.

Explaining to others

Can the outcome arrived at be *explained to others* in such a way that they are *convinced* that the solution is sound? For such a *communication to be valid,* pupils may have to use instructions, diagrams, etc, using oral, written or pictorial methods, including technological means.

Having presented the arguments to others, has the pupil *proved* that the solution is sound? This final stage allows others to question and criticise any arguments heard. This affords the presenter the opportunity of having a rudimentary analysis carried out in a friendly environment.

Problem solving within Century Maths

As an aid to pupils acquiring problem-solving strategies, a selection of problem-solving activities is built into the *Teacher's Support Packs*. Some of the activities selected are taken from the Theme/Focus material and extended to include illustrations on how to develop a number of the strategies listed above. In this way, teachers are able to observe how Century Maths supports these strategic skills.

From its inception, Century Maths has been developed from a problem-solving standpoint. In both Theme and Focus books Century Maths provides many opportunities to use and develop problem-solving skills. The situations provided will act as a springboard for the pupils to consider further situations. These new situations will, in turn, give rise to many problems requiring resolution.

Keeping the records straight

What do we need to record?

How does the pupil's work fit into the record?

Record-keeping needs to be a constructive activity. How can we achieve this?

Who are we keeping the record for?

How can I find the time to produce all these records?

How often should the recording be done?

Can the pupils take more responsibility for keeping records?

Keeping a record of record of progress and achievement for each pupil is a central area of teacher assessment. Without a sound record-keeping mechanism, capable of providing evidence to substantiate a teacher's professional judgment, the assessment of each pupil will lose credibility. However, there is no one correct way to achieve this – each school has unique requirements, and every teacher must have a clear understanding of the aims behind any agreed system adopted by the school. Such a system must be:

- unobtrusive within the teaching environment;
- seen by pupils and teachers alike to be a positive activity;
- easily manageable for the teacher and not a time-consuming exercise.

Record-keeping within Century Maths attempts to satisfy these three major criteria. Essentially, each pupil is given a simple four-part assessment record, which he or she completes regularly. The teacher adds comments and suggestions to this. The four parts of the assessment record are the Record of Achievement, the Action Report, the Review and the Summary (see pages 11–14).

In order to illustrate fully how Century Maths record-keeping satisfies the three criteria stated, the questions posed at the beginning of this section are answered in detail below.

What do we need to record?

Century Maths recording concentrates on observable evidence, gained from the classroom situation. It contains a pupil's initial reactions to the Theme material (see Record of Achievement, page 11). This is then followed up with on-going pupil comments relating to daily/weekly progess with notes referring to allied Focus materials used (see Action report). The teacher makes comments at regular intervals on the Record of Achievement, having negotiated with the pupil what will be written down. Such comments may include specific references to some areas of mathematics handled successfully or with difficulty, as well as more general comments.

How does the pupil's work fit into the record?

At the end of each Theme, pupils complete the sections on the Review relating to their feelings about the work on Theme and Focus materials and how they think they have progressed. Teachers will then make a summative statement about the pupils' work during the Theme on the Summary, possibly using pupils' work as substantiation of the comments made.

Record-keeping needs to be a constructive activity. How can we achieve this?

This is achieved in Century Maths by providing a method of record-keeping which:

- is flexible;

- is easy to use;
- is meaningful to the pupils and teachers;
- acknowledges the activities which pupils have been involved in – and not only those within the context of the National Curriculum;
- contains evidence of work produced by the pupils;
- is integrated into the work being carried out;
- provides a method of supplying cross-curricular evidence;
- involves discussion between pupils and teachers.

Who are we keeping the record for?

- The pupils: to give a sense of ownership of their work as well as ensuring a sense of progress;
- the teacher: to assist in planning and to inform about the success (or otherwise) of a teaching strategy, while at the same time, through regular communication with the pupils, increasing the teacher's knowledge of each pupil;
- the next teacher;
- the pupil's parents;
- the head teacher and the governing body;
- whoever is monitoring the National Curriculum.

How can I find the time to produce all these records?

Century Maths record-keeping is an integral part of the classroom environment. It merges into the teacher's observation of and interaction with the pupil in the classroom. It supports the learning and teaching, facilitates pupil progress and continuity, but does not encroach upon the activities in hand.

Can the pupils take more responsibility for keeping records?

Clearly, the Century Maths model of record-keeping places pupil involvement at the very heart of the activity. All records are 'pupil-driven' with the teacher monitoring and commenting when appropriate. Assessment is from both parties, with pupil comments relating to their own feelings about the progress being achieved, as well as teacher comments relating to a variety of activities observed.

How often should the recording be done?

The record can be filled in by teachers as and when they deem it necessary, but generally about once a week. The most appropriate time for teachers to talk to the pupils about their comments is when both parties feel it would be most beneficial.

But ... I think I need a checklist to keep me up to date with each of my pupils.

Although Century Maths does not subscribe to a checklist mode of record-keeping, perhaps some schools or departments may require such a list as part of the overall assessment procedure. Teachers could develop a checklist based on the Focus coverage indicated within the pupil records. It could serve to:

- build up an overview related to the attainment targets (but this should be only one reason for keeping records);

- indicate where the 'gaps' are appearing in coverage of Focus material;

- show the 'spread' of levels being tackled by each pupil. A possible model for such a checklist is provided (see Pupil summary page).

However, you should be aware that such a checklist:

- indicates coverage and not necessarily achievement;

- is not evidence of a pupil's progress, merely an indication of what was observed on a particular day;

- may give the false impression that you are only interested in National Curriculum attainment targets.

Fine, but why has Century Maths developed its record-keeping and assessment around the pupils?

There are many reasons why we have decided to do this, some more important than others. Some of our reasons you may disagree with. We consider that pupil involvement in record-keeping:

- encourages pupils to have a sense of ownership over their own work;

- increases pupils' awareness of the very nature of mathematics;

- allows pupils to observe and understand their progress and the continuity within Century Maths;

- heightens pupils' awareness of their own achievements and development;

- develops pupils' understanding of where their mathematics fits within a cross-curricular framework;

- enables pupils to identify their own strengths and weaknesses;

- develops pupils' reflective and analytical skills.

This list not in order of priority, nor is it exhaustive, but it does indiate a firm belief in an active role for all pupils in their own assessment.

Do we always have to base our judgments on written evidence?

Teachers are the best people to assess their own pupils. They will be aware of what guidance has been given and how pupils have responded to a variety of situations. This essential information forms the central part of any assessment and can be gleaned from observation, discussion and questioning, or any other interaction, including a written response.

But how can we assess an individual's input within a group situation?

Here, many general strategies are available. It is important to select suitable strategies for providing the most useful and reliable evidence, without distorting the task in hand. Consider:

- general observation of the group dynamics;
- discussion with the whole group as a natural part of the activity;
- discussion with individuals during and after the task;
- individually-completed written reports;
- group evaluations of each person's involvement and input.

Through the Century maths record sheets, the individual pupils' involvement within any group activity should become more apparent.

And how can we assess the application of their mathematics effectively?

The application of mathematics underpins all the attainment targets. It represents essential aspects of *all* mathematical activities. It is, therefore, not desirable to assess this separately. However, if you consider the assessment of the application of mathematics appropriate, you should focus on three essential strands of pupils' mathematical development, allowing a possible fourth strand (extension) for differentiation at the higher levels.

These three strands are:

- task management
- communication
- mathematical insight.

Under these three strands (or four with the extension strand added) a criteria matrix can be created.

Such a matrix should be used bearing in mind the teacher's knowledge of the pupils and the way the pupils have worked. This is essential if effective assessment is to take place.

One example of a criteria matrix is given overleaf. When using such a grid, a number of questions must be addressed:

- is 'observed once' sufficient evidence to record a pupil's progress in terms of a level descriptor?
- What method do we adopt to moderate a pupil's work seen to be at different levels for different strands of the matrix?
- What role does the 'Extension' column play – if any – in the overall assessment of a pupil's work?

Having considered these and many other questions, we hope that the matrix will be some assistance when you come to consider each activity to be assessed within the Theme material.

Criteria Matrix for the Application of Mathematics

Level	Task Management	Mathematical Insight	Communication	Extension
3	Select materials and mathematics	Offer evidence of understanding Check results	Explain work in clear manner	Make and test some simple predictions
4	Select appropriate materials from given resources Show evidence of methodical planning	Test patterns observed	Use appropriate method to record results	Use examples to test statements
5	Make request for the appropriate materials Plan for full information	Check patterns and calculations Suggest possible outcomes	Interpret the given information	Make and test statements relating to the task in hand
6	Design a task and select appropriate equipment and mathematics Obtain all required information	Record and test findings with accuracy Show evidence of 'trial and improvement' methods	Present findings in oral, written or visual form	Make and test generalisations and hypotheses
7	Devise a mathematical task Decide upon an agreed structure	Work methodically within the agreed structure Use 'trial and improvement' methods Follow a chain of mathematical reasoning, spotting inconsistencies	Review progress and present findings in an appropriate manner	Follow new investigation using some alternative approaches
8	Devise a mathematical task Make a detailed plan of the work	Work methodically through the task Check information for completeness Consider the results in the light of the original task	Present findings in a coherent manner State evidence of reasons for making chosen decisions	Conjecturise using such statements as: 'If . . . then . . .' define, reason, prove and disprove
9	Design and plan a mathematical task	Consider and state conjectures and show whether true, false or not proven. Evidence of the use of counter examples Reach a successful conclusion	Be able to define and reason through the task Interpret findings clearly	Use symbolisation Recognise and use 'necessary and sufficient' condition
10	Design and plan a mathematical task	Use symbolisation with confidence Reach a successful conclusion	Present alternative solutions Justify with evidence the route selected	Give definitions which are sufficient or minimal Construct a proof by contradiction

Guide to the completion of Century Maths record sheets

Record of achievement

Name:

Class:

Theme/Focus:

Start date:

Main activity

A simple description of what the pupil intends to do, which could be explained better later in the project

First ideas

What we are going to do?

'Brainstorming' kind of response after discussion in a whole class group and smaller group

On-going opportunity to record Focus maths links

Other activities

To be added to as the Theme develops

T

Suggestions by teacher, helpful notes, positive comments

Action report

Name:

Class:

Theme/Focus:

Finishing date:

Week	What we achieved	[Theme/Focus] Note made of linked Focus Work	[Theme/Focus] Note made of computer work	Comment How is your work progressing? Any major problems? Are you enjoying the Theme/Focus materials? What would you like help with?
1	Factual record of what has been completed or started	Note made of linked Focus Work	Note made of computer work	On-going self-assessment and evaluation, with the statements made being a helpful guide for discussion between pupil and teacher the following week
2				
3				
4				
5				
6				

© Stanley Thornes (Publishers) Ltd 1991   **Century Maths**

Review – Looking back . . .

CenturyMATHS

Name: _____ **Class:** _____

Theme/Focus: _____

Week 1 2 3 4 5 6

Are you pleased with your work on the Theme/Focus materials? Which parts went well?

Positive achievements

Group members:

Note of who has been working with the pupil

How well did you work together?

Co-operative skills tackled

What have you learned during your work on the Theme/Focus materials?

Hopefully, statements relating to Attainment Targets 1 and 9 might emerge

Which maths caused you some difficulty?

Targets for the future

Which parts of the Theme/Focus materials did you not enjoy?

Negative aspects opened up so that the teacher can talk these through

How could you have improved your work?

Targets for the future

How did your computer work go?

Importance of information technology skills stressed

Which maths links did you do?

Connections with Focus units

Summary

Name: _____ **Class:** _____

Theme/Focus: _____ [Theme/Focus puzzle piece] **Date:** _____

Main activities

Theme:

Summary by pupil

Focus:

Achievements

National Curriculum Attainment Targets covered/levels attained/ areas of mathematics involved

Some sort of teacher assessment or simply work covered

Pupil comment:

Opportunies for improved communication between pupils, teachers and parents

Teacher comment:

Opportunities for improved communication between pupils, teachers and parents

Parent comment:

Opportunities for improved communication between pupils, teachers and parents

Year 7/8 Pupil summary page

Name:	Class:

Handling data

Units

	1	2	3	4	5	6	7	8	9	10	11			
Lead-in	1	2	3	4	5	6	7	8	9	10	11			
Core	1	2	3	4	5	6	7	8	9	10	11			
Extension	1	2	3	4	5	6	7	8	9	10	11	12	13	14

Number

Units

	1	2	3	4	5	6	7	8	9	10	11	12
Lead-in	1	2	3	4	5	6	7					
Core	1	2	3	4	5	6	7	8	9	10	11	12
Extension	1	2	3	4	5	6	7	8	9	10	11	12

Shape and space

Units

	1	2	3	4	5	6	7	8	9	10	11
Lead-in	1	2	3	4	5	6	7	8	9	10	
Core	1	2	3	4	5	6	7	8	9	10	
Extension	1	2	3	4	5	6	7	8	9	10	11

Algebra

Units

	1	2	3	4	5	6	7	8	9	10	11	12	13	14	15
Lead-in	1	2	3	4	5	6	7	8	9	10	11				
Core	1	2	3	4	5	6	7	8	9	10	11	12			
Extension	1	2	3	4	5	6	7	8	9						

Theme

Animals · Trees · Neighbourhood · School fair · Festivals · Ourselves · Patterns · Traffic · Holidays · Connections · Music · Food

At the end of each half term, shade in Themes and Focus units you have worked on.

Equipment and materials for Century Maths

The basket of equipment

 This 'basket' contains all the general equipment and materials we would expect to be available in the classroom at all times for working on **Century Maths**:

calculators
compasses
felt tips
glue sticks
pencils
protractors
rubbers
rulers
scissors

sellotape
staplers
plain paper
graph paper
1 cm square and
    1 cm isometric grid paper
1 cm square and
    1 cm isometric dotty paper
tracing paper

More specific equipment and materials, required for a particular task in a Theme section or Focus unit, are shown on the relevant spreads in the pupil books and the *Teachers's Support Packs*. These fall into two categories:

✔ equipment and materials that you *will* need

○ equipment and materials that you *may* need

Flagging of activities in pupils' texts

Theme books

▭ highlights key activity(ies) on page

● supplementary activity(ies), often optional, or series of stages in an activity

▶ more ideas based on the same topic

Focus books

■ a pupil activity

☐ activity with pupil-generated answer – no answer/solution given in *Teacher's Support Pack*

2 activity for which answer/solution is given in *Teacher's Support Pack*

Y 7/8 Number – Lead-In: summary of units

Unit titles	Activities	Materials required	NC NATs (PoS) Levels	Teacher notes on scope for maths development
1 **Using whole numbers** *Pages 2 – 10*	*Number recognition activities* *Estimation* *Games* *Investigations* *Calculator work*	✓ 🗔 *1, 3* *Counters* *A dice* ▣ **LN** *B1* ✓ 🗔 *2* *Light card* *Pointed sticks, pencils or matchsticks* ▢	**NAT 2** *2a, b, c, d, g; 3a, b* **NAT 3** *2b*	
2 **Problems with numbers** *Pages 11 – 19*	*Activities based on calculator usage*	▢	**NAT 2** *2f; 3b, c, d* **NAT 3** *2b; 3b*	
3 **Using fractions** *Pages 20 – 26*	*Practical activities for introducing fractions*	✓ 🗔 *4 – 7* *Coin* *Different coloured counters* *A die* ○ *Coloured paper* ▢	**NAT 2** *2f; 4j*	
4 **All about money** *Pages 27 – 36*	*Activities about money:* *Investigational activities* *Games* *Problem solving activities* *Consolidation activities*	✓ 🗔 *8, 9* *Prices of food items* *Dice* *Counters*	**NAT 2** *2d, e; 3d, e, h*	
5 **Measuring** *Pages 37 – 49*	*Activities to build up experience of estimation and correct units*	✓ 🗔 *10* *Metre rule or tape measure* *Silent clock or watch with seconds* *Textbook* *Weighing scales* *Wire* *Large elastic band* *Staples* *Card* *Weights* ▢	**NAT 2** *3f, j, k* **NAT 4** *2f*	
6 **More problems with numbers** *Pages 50 – 60*	*Consolidation number activities*	✓ 🗔 *11 – 13* *Playing cards* ○ *Matchsticks* *Square plastic tiles* ▢	**NAT 3** *2a; 3b*	
7 **Below zero** *Pages 61 – 64*	*An introduction to directed numbers, through reading scales and playing games*	✓ 🗔 *14 – 18* *Thermometers* *Newspapers* *Travel brochures* *Counters* *Paper clips*	**NAT 2** *3i, k* **NAT 3** *3b*	

Unit 1 Using whole numbers

Activities

Materials required

Wriggle to it

  1

Counter for each player
Dice

Spinner scores

  2

Light card
Printed sticks or pencils or matchsticks

Estimation games

  3

Numbers database

   LN B1

Computing references

Grouping in tens

Use of Logo for number stacks

See **LP** A4.

Number database

Use of computers for 'Numbers database'

See **LN** B1.

Teaching suggestions

This unit is based on number recognition activities, estimation, games, investigations and calculator work.

Wriggle to it

This has been included to give pupils the experience of adding on and taking away by employing a counting forwards and backwards strategy. Errors can be made by pupils if they employ a wrong counting strategy, e.g. when the counter is on three and the next throw is four, pupils will land on six, seven or eight. As seven is correct, with six the pupil has counted the starting position and with eight has not realised when to finish. If misconceptions are noted, further work can be done with simple household games.

Numbers in figures

This links numbers written in words and figures. If a mistake has been made, pupils can see it and check for themselves.

Grouping in tens

This activity is designed as an easy beginning to place value. It can be used to *assess* whether pupils have attached any meaning to the digits. It has been extended to use the RANDOM function in Logo.

Juggle a number

This extends the place value to include hundreds. It is extended through investigation to considering the different combinations using 3 digits, and building up further. The activity encourages pattern finding and, perhaps, a rule.

Spinner scores

The activity requires a pupil to work systematically. Pupils should be encouraged to commit their work to paper when making spinners with their own numbers. Teachers can ask questions such as 'What rules are you going to have?' 'Which numbers have you decided to use?'

Spotty looks

Looking at odd and even numbers is the focus of this activity.

Estimation games

Here the emphasis is on the help needed for those with a poor sense of 'how many' unless things are grouped conventionally, e.g. in twos, fives, tens.

Scattered objects are more difficult but here the pupil can check by counting later.

Crowds

This is an extension of 'Estimation games'.

Number database

This is an activity in which pupils explore one number at a time and record their findings.

. . . Using whole numbers

Answers

Page 3

12 + 90 + 32 + 50 + 17	= 201	Agrees
5 + 8 + 16 + 2 + 20	= 51	Disagrees
23 + 69 + 17 + 60	= 169	Disagrees

Page 4

1

	0-9	10-19	20-29	30-39	40-49	50-59	60-69	70-79	80-89	90-99
		(17)		(32)						
	(0)	(15)	(25)	39				(76)		
	(4)	16	25	39		(53)	(69)	70	(86)	
	8	15	23	36	44	59	64	76	87	92

2   Ringed numbers above in 1

Page 5

1   359   395   539   593   935   953
     6 different numbers
2   953
3   95
4   24
5   9853
6   3589

Page 7

1   7, 8
2   2 in each
3

  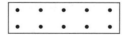

4   22, 14, 26, 20, 38

Page 9

1   120 would be a reasonable estimate.
2   170

Page 10

1

1 1 x 1 square	6 2 x 3 rectangle
2 1 x 2 prime	7 1 x 7 prime
3 1 x 3 prime	8 2 x 2 x 2 cube
4 2 x 2 square	9 3 x 3 square
5 1 x 5 prime	10 2 x 5 rectangle

2

11 1 x 11 prime	16 2 x 2 x 2 x 2 square
12 2 x 2 x 3 rectangle	17 1 x 17 prime
13 1 x 13 prime	18 2 x 3 x 3 rectangle
14 2 x 7 rectangle	19 1 x 19 prime
15 3 x 5 rectangle	20 2 x 2 x 5 rectangle

Links with National Curriculum Attainment Targets: Programmes of Study level descriptors

NAT	Level	PoS Descriptor(s)
2	2	a, b, c, d, g
	3	a, b
3	2	b

Unit **2** Problems with numbers

Activities

Materials required

▢ Computing references

Number chains

Use of spreadsheet to set up a rule

See **S** **LN** S3

Codes

Use of Logotron Logo to extend work

Links with National Curriculum Attainment Targets: Programmes of Study level descriptors

NAT	Level	PoS Descriptor(s)
2	2	f
	3	b, c, d
3	2	b
	3	b

Teaching suggestions

This unit includes a lot of activities based around the use of calculators.

Speeding up

This is an activity to encourage pupils to look at different ways of working out various sums and *discussing* the quickest way. There should be some recognition that multiplying is a quick way to add the same number together.

Four figures

This provides an early introduction to the calculator. The activity can be done as a group. Further rules can be made up by the pupils, e.g. 'Can we put two numbers together?' – 2 and 3 become 23. An extension of this work is to have different calculators which use different logic so that the need for brackets can be explored.

Sloppy Joe's homework

'Sloppy Joe' activities can be used *diagnostically*. Pupils do not always interpret the two division signs in the conventional manner. The difficulty arises because of the different language assigned to division: 'goes into', 'shares by', 'divided by', 'divided into'.

This exercise is best done by a group or a whole class. When the first four have been done by the majority of the class, pupils can be stopped and answers compared. Agreement needs to be reached on how each of these statements is read. Writing down the rules will act as a reminder of the agreements reached. It is a part of this task that the pupils realise the importance of everyone reading the rules in the same way.

The second activity is intended as a check on previous work on division and can be used as an assessment task to find out if more help is required or the work has been understood.

Number chain

'Number chain' is another investigation based on odd and even numbers. The pupils are encouraged to develop this further using different numbers and rules.

Codes

'Codes' provide practice on addition, using number codes in a creative way. The work can be extended by using Logo.

Calculator words

This has been included to allow pupils to get to know their calculators in a fun way. The extension is to get them to make up some of their own. This is a challenge firstly because they have no clues as to the initial exercise, and secondly they have to think of a sum to suit their answers.

Number paths

This is a check on pupils' understanding of simple multiplication facts. Designed this way, the pupils can spot whether or not they have made mistakes: if they find their message does not make sense, something is wrong!

. . . **Problems with numbers**

Answers

Page 11

1. $4 + 4 + 4 + 4 + 4 = 4 \times 5 = 20$
    $9 + 9 + 9 + 9 + 9 + 9 + 9 = 9 \times 7 = 63$
    $40 - 5 - 5 - 5 - 5 - 5 = 40 - (5 \times 5) = 15$

2. $17 \times 5 = 85$
    $25 \times 7 = 175$
    641

3. See above

Page 12

1. Possible answers include:

1	$2 - 1$	6	3×2	11	$4 \times 3 - 1$	16	4×4
2	$1 + 1$	7	$4 \times 2 - 1$	12	4×3	17	$4 \times 4 + 1$
3	$2 + 1$	8	4×2	13	$6 \times 2 + 1$	18	6×3
4	2×2	9	3×3	14	7×2	19	$6 \times 3 + 1$
5	$3 + 2$	10	2×5	15	5×3	20	5×4

2. See above

Page 13

1. $56 + 56 + 56 + \ldots$ 47 times or $47 + 47 + 47 + \ldots$ 56 times
2. $(50 \times 56) - (3 \times 56)$ 3. $47 \times 57 - 47$
4. $13 \times ? = 182$ Trial and error to find?

Page 14

1. $16 \div 8 = 2$ $8\overline{)16} = 2$ $15 \div 5 = 3$ $24 \div 8 = 3$
    $3\overline{)24} = 8$ $5\overline{)10} = 2$ $4\overline{)12} = 3$ $12 \div 3 = 4$

Page 15

1. $10\overline{)2} = 0.2$ $5 \div 10 = 0.5$ $16 \div 4 = 4$ $4 \div 16 = 0.25$
    $10 \div 5 = 2$ $16\overline{)4} = 0.25$ $4\overline{)16} = 4$

2. $8 \div 16 = 0.5$ $6 \div 24 = 0.25$ $16 \div 8 = 2$ $10 \div 100 = 0.1$
    $24\overline{)6} = 0.25$ $8\overline{)16} = 2$ $6\overline{)24} = 4$
    $16\overline{)8} = 0.5$ $24 \div 6 = 4$ $100\overline{)10} = 0.1$

Page 17

1. $32 + 16 + 8 = 56$
    $128 + 64 + 32 + 8 + 4 + 2 + 1 = 239$
    $8 + 1 = 9$
    $16 + 8 = 24$

Page 18

1. LCD displays:
    LEO   HOBO   LEGS   SHOES   GOOSE

Page 19

1.
Clue		Clue		Clue	
1	20	5	70	9	35
2	30	6	20	10	80
3	20	7	15	11	0
4	45	8	25	12	10

2. DO THE NEXT PAGE

2. 128 64 32 16 8 4 2 1
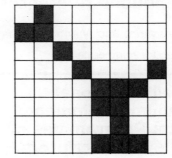

Unit 3 Using fractions

Activities

Materials required

Triominoes and quarters

 Coloured paper

Shade it

  4

Halves and quarters

  5

Coin, Different coloured counter for each player, A dice

Halving a square

  6

Fraction dominoes

  7

☐ Computing references

Halving a square and Number halving

Use of Logo for number halving

Links with National Curriculum Attainment Targets: Programmes of Study level descriptors

NAT	Level	PoS Descriptor(s)
2	2	f
	4	j

Teaching suggestions

The whole unit introduces fractions in a practical way.

Triominoes

Triominoes gives a practical experience of halves, thirds and quarters. This has been included because most early experience of fractions given to pupils is of the sort that enables them to count squares to obtain correct answers, i.e. colour a quarter of this shape. There are only four parts to this shape so they are only required to shade one part of the whole shape.

Shade it

This is really a case of consolidation but this time in the form of a game. Pupils can be encouraged, if necessary, to record what they have coloured in after each throw of the die –

e.g. $\frac{1}{4}$:   or

Halves and quarters

This is a motivating exercise on multiplying fractions and whole numbers. Pupils can use diagrams to help them work out the answers if they feel this will help.

Halving a square

This forms an initial introduction to halving. Pupils will have to consider what rules are allowed, i.e. each shape can only have whole squares or the squares can be divided up as well. The two halves must be made up of connecting squares. Whatever rules they choose must be kept with the 3 × 3 and 5 × 5 pupils' squares. Can they find any patterns in their results?

Halving a rectangle

This is an extension and separate exercise.

Fraction dominoes

A game which allows pupils to look at equivalence of fractions.

Number halving

The final activity in this unit, 'Number halving', involves using Logo to halve whole numbers. This can be linked to the number chains in Unit 1. It can be extended to quartering, doubling.

. . . Using fractions

Answers

Page 23

1. By ensuring that eight squares are in each part.
2. There are many ways of doing this.
   Check that 1, above, holds in each case.
3. As with 2, 3 x 3 should have
   4.5 squares in each part.
   5 x 5 should have 12.5 squares in each part.
4. Differing shapes need to be checked individually.

Page 24

1. 2 x 3 should have 3 squares in each part.
3. 2 x 4 gives 4 in each part.
   2 x 5 gives 5 in each part.
   2 x 6 gives 6 in each part.
4. Each half contains the same number of squares as the
   length of the rectangle.

Activities

Materials required

Weekend budget

 Prices of items of food

Double dice

 Pair of dice

Look for your pocket money

  8
Counter for each player
A dice

Balance your pocket money

  9
Counter for each player
A dice

▢ Computing references

Links with National Curriculum Attainment Targets: Programmes of Study level descriptors

NAT	Level	PoS Descriptor(s)
2	2	d, e
	3	d, e, h

Teaching suggestions

This unit on money is predominantly investigational but also includes games, problem-solving activities and consolidation exercises.

How much?

The first activity is an investigation using any four coins the pupils choose. Some pupils will find a pattern within which to work, while others will need guidance to avoid duplicating their answers.

Bus fares and No change

'Bus fares' and 'No change' are two related activities. Both are investigational and based on bus fares. The first asks pupils to choose four coins and decide which fares could be paid. This is extended to five coins. Pupils have to decide which selection of coins would be best.

'No change' is a problem-solving activity based on sorting out change and fares.

Weekend budget

This is a very open activity drawing on the pupils' experience of spending and also planning a budget – in this case based on £10. This activity will need a good deal of research in finding out prices. It can be extended to a project on best buys: e.g. an eight oz can of beans costs 36p; a six oz can costs 28p. Which is the best buy?

Sweet packs

This is a consolidation of the previous exercise put into a problem-solving activity.

Double dice

This activity is a game in the context of a school fete. It provides more practice in the addition of money. Pupils should be encouraged to play several times and to write down the results. It can be extended by getting the pupils to re-organise the game to increase the profit.

Crafty Aunty or Aunty Crafty

Aunty Crafty's letter enables pupils to explore three different ways of inheriting money. They have to consider each of the three ways, decide which way is best and why.

Look for your pocket money!

This is a game for two or more to consolidate addition of money. Pupils can extend the game by changing the rules or by developing the game to include some subtraction.

Snack machine

This is another problem-solving activity based on calculations involved in making selection.

. . . All about money

Teaching Suggestions

Balance your pocket money

This is another game but one that brings out several misconceptions:

1. Answers must be positive.
2. In subtracting, smaller minus bigger is either not possible or is the same if reversed.
3. Adding increases number in absolute terms.

Each pupil will need a balance sheet and a counter. Each pair of children will need a money line and one die per game. The target is to get £50 credit.

Each pupil starts with £20 on their money line. Each takes it in turn to throw the die and act on the instructions in the square on which they land. Players mark up their own balance sheets and opponents keep a check on the entries using the money line. Some pupils will enjoy making a money game of their own.

Answers

Page 28

1   1p; 2p; 3p; 4p; 21p; 22p; 23p; 24p

Page 29

1   Bianca gives Amin 50p. Courtney gives Amin £1 and he in turn gives Courtney 50p.
2   Amin pays £1.20, then Bianca gives Amin 40p (1 x 20p and 2 x 10p). Courtney gives Amin £1 and he in turn gives Courtney 60p (1 x 50p and 1 x 10p).

Page 31

1   12p   2   Kit Kat : 22p   Twix : 17p

Page 32

1   Yes

Page 35

1   Crisps : (10p, 5p) (10p, 2p, 2p, 1p)
     Sweets : (2p, 2p) (2p, 1p, 1p) (1p, 1p, 1p, 1p)
     Nuts : (10p) (5p, 5p) (5p, 2p, 2p, 1p)
     Chockbar : (10p, 2p) (5p, 5p, 2p) (10p, 1p, 1p)
     Orange : (10p, 5p, 2p) (5p, 5p, 5p, 2p)
     Cake : (20p) (10p, 10p) (10p, 5p, 5p) (5p, 5p, 5p, 5p)
     Raisins : (10p, 5p, 1p) (5p, 5p, 5p, 1p) (10p, 2p, 2p, 2p)
     Toffees : (10p, 5p, 2p, 1p)
     Bombay Mix : (10p, 2p, 1p) (5p, 5p, 2p, 1p)

2
Crisps	Sweets	Nuts	Chockbar	Orange	Cake	Raisins	Toffees	Bombay Mix
2	3	3	3	2	4	3	1	2

3   10p, 5p, 2p, 2p
4   Combinations of Nuts (5p, 5p), Chockbar (10p, 2p) and Cake (10p, 10p).
5   A Cake (20p) and Nuts (10p) with any of Chockbar, Crisps and Sweets.

Unit 5 Measuring

Activities

Materials required

Estimating in your classroom

 Metre rule or tape measure

Clock it

 Silent clock or watch with seconds

Estimating heights

 Metre rule or tape measure
Textbook

Estimating weights

 Weighing scales

Weighing light things

 Kitchen weighing scales

Make your own spring balance

 Weighing scales, Wire, Large elastic band, Staples, Card, Weights

Teaching suggestions

This Measuring unit relies upon building up experience of estimation and correct units. Preliminary work on this unit can be use of non-standard measuring.

Can you tell?

In the first activity pupils have to make decisions about the accuracy of other people's estimates of lengths. During the activity, they are asked to make statements for themselves to share with a partner.

Estimating in your classroom and Estimating heights

These activities allow pupils the opportunity to choose lengths, heights and widths within their environment. They will also encourage the use of appropriate measures. They are further extended by pupils comparing their estimates with those of others, using spreadsheets. The estimates are then checked by making measurements, using the most appropriate units.

Clock it

This is a practical game for estimating time.

Estimating weights

This activity is based on observation of everyday objects followed by a practical activity. Discussion is likely to involve stones, pounds, kilograms. Accurate reading of the measuring instruments should be ensured by adjusting the instruments before use.

Measuring light things

This is a move from estimation of weights to actual weighing. The extension given is an activity about how to find the weight of very light things by finding the weight of many and then dividing to find the weight of one.

Make your own spring balance

This activity is about pupils devising their own spring balance. Pupils should be encouraged to follow the activity as they find it developing – e.g. what difference do different thicknesses of elastic bands make? Tabulation of results should be clear.

Measuring scales

This activity raises pupils' awareness of mistakes that can be made when they are reading different scales. As an extension, pupils can be encouraged to write down rules for reading scales.

A million!

Here pupils explore 1 000 000 seconds, pages, people, grains of rice. It allows them to explore the size, length, time of 1 000 000.

. . . **Measuring**

Clocks

This activity uses both 12-hour and 24-hour clocks to display time. The pupils are asked to think about what they do at certain times of the day. An extension would be to plan a journey using public transport and real timetable data.

What did you do yesterday? and Guess-times

These explore the time and duration of pupils' activities.

All change

This is a consolidation exercise on different measures.

Answers

Page 37

1. A daffodil is about 30 cm high.
   An apple is about 10 cm across.
   This book is about 20 cm wide.
   A fly is about 1 cm long.
2. A knife handle is about 10 cm long.
   Our teacher is about 1.8 m tall.
   A car is about 5 m long.
   The classroom is about 10 m long.
   This book is about 2 cm thick.

Page 41

1. Feather, leaf, grape, tomato, banana, apple, jam.
   There will be discussion about large/small fruit!
2. Apple and banana, leaf and feather, possibly.

Page 44

1. Joe has forgotten the fact that the girl is taller than 1 m.
   Hence he should be saying 'You're 1.58 m high.'
   The ruler has not been placed so that 0 cm is at the edge of the book. The correct comment is 'This book is nearly 10 cm wide.'
   The ruler has not been placed so that 0 cm is at the edge of the plate. The correct comment is 'It's exactly 5 cm wide.'
1. A = 3 kg   B = 14 kg   C = 56 kg   D = 68 kg
   E = 99.4°F   F = 96.2°F   G = 94.8°F
   H = 20 mph   I = 35 mph   J = 55 mph
   K = 67.5 mph L = 81 mph   M = 94 mph

Page 45

1. 10 km high
2. Approximately 1500 km
3. Approximately 12 days
4. Approximately 12.5 kg

Page 46

1. Yes

Page 49

2. The parcel weighs 15 kg not 12½ kg.
   The old clock is 10 minutes fast, not 9 minutes fast.
   The change should be £1.25, not £2.25.

Materials required

Clocks

 10

Guess-times

Watch with seconds

▢ Computing references

Estimating in your classroom and *Estimating heights*

Use of spreadsheets for comparing estimates

See **S** **LN** S1, S4

A million!

Use of computer to count up to a million

Links with National Curriculum Attainment Targets: Programmes of Study level descriptors

NAT	Level	PoS Descriptor(s)
2	3	f, j, k
4	2	f

Unit 6 More problems with numbers

Activities

Materials required

Jump to it

  11,12

Card numbers

 Playing cards

Matchstick patterns (1) and (2)

 Matchsticks

Fishponds and *Patterns in paving slabs*

 Square plastic tiles

Number trails

  13

⬜ Computing references

Matchstick patterns (1) and (2)

Fishponds

Seats and tables

Patterns in paving slabs

Use of spreadsheets

See S LN S3

Teaching suggestions

This unit is a collection of investigations to allow consolidation of earlier work as well as allowing the teacher to assess basic work. There is strong emphasis on AT1.

Jump to it

This is another way of looking at work with tables. Pupils do not have to stop after going round the circles once; and they can enlarge the circles to include more dots or use worksheet 12 which has rings with different numbers of dots.

Card numbers

Another challenge. What numbers can be made using 1, 3 and 5? Deliberately there are no rules, so pupils can combine the numbers, e.g. 1 and 5 can become 15. What numbers cannot be made? What happens when three other numbers are chosen?

This activity can be used over a wide ability level where pupils may explore buttons on the calculator.

Matchsticks (1) and (2)

Matchsticks, like materialistic patterns, are familiar investigations in which pupils can predict the next number and try to produce rules for a larger number of matchsticks.

Fishponds

This investigation requires pupils to count the slabs around the edge of ponds. They should be encouraged to start with the three ponds on the page and then to draw some more for themselves. Dotty or square grid paper would be helpful.

The results can be put into a table. Pupils are encouraged by the activity to look for a pattern in their results. Asking them to predict some of the next results and then drawing them is a good strategy for solving such problems.

This activity can be given to pupils of a wide range of ability, and the processes and outcomes assessed. Some will only be able to draw out the ponds, others may be able to work out a formula, in words or algebraically.

A further extension would be to consider non-square ponds.

Seats and tables

This is an investigation which requires pupils to count as well as to be systematic in their approach. Not much guidance has been given on how to proceed. Pupils may wish to draw out the different arrangements, or put their results in a table.

The activity already includes an extension by showing another way the tables may be arranged and inviting the pupils to choose the best arrangement and explain why. It is suggested that they may like to consider other ways for themselves.

... More problems with numbers

Patterns in paving slabs

An investigation which gives a practical experience of counting and working systematically. It is extended by considering other layouts.

Perimeters (1) and (2)

An investigation on perimeters and counting. With the starting example, pupils keep a constant area of four squares and change the perimeter. What conclusions can they draw from their results? This activity is extended in the next task, by exploring triangles.

Number trails

This game has been designed to mix all four basic rules. Any errors pupils make will show up if they do not reach the answer 12. They can then move on to try other starting numbers and then be encouraged to make up their own number trails and challenge a partner.

Links with National Curriculum Attainment Targets: Programmes of Study level descriptors

NAT	Level	PoS Descriptor(s)
3	2	a
	3	b

Answers

Page 50

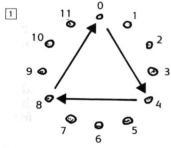 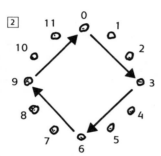

3. Jumps of 1, 5, 7, 11 use all of the stones.

Page 52

2.

Number of squares in row	1	2	3	4
Number of matches	4	7	10	13

3.

Squares	20	25	30	36	40	48	100
Matches	61	76	91	109	121	145	301

4. Without using notation, pupils should express $3n + 1$ where n is the number of squares.

5. 333

Page 53

1.

Triangles	1	2	3	4
Matches	3	5	7	9

2. In pupils' own words, $2n + 1$ where n is the number of triangles.

3. 201

. . . **More problems with numbers**

Page 54

[1] 8   [2] 12   [3] 16

[7]

Size of pond (n for n x n)	1	2	3	4	5	8	10	12
Number of square slabs	8	12	16	20	24	36	44	52

[8] Using their own words, pupils should explain 4n + 4 where n is the size of the side of the square.

Page 55

[1] 22 chairs   [2] 34 chairs   [3] 7 tables
[4] 4n + 2 where n is the number of tables.   [5] 2n + 4

Page 56

[1]

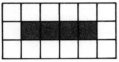

[2] 14

[3]

Layout	Number of brown slabs	Number of white slabs
1	1	8
2	2	10
3	3	12
4	4	14
5	5	16
6	6	18
7	7	20
8	8	22
9	9	24
10	10	26

[4] 46 white slabs

[5] 22 brown slabs

Page 57

[9]

Layout	Number of brown slabs	Number of white slabs
1	1	8
2	3	12
3	5	16
1	1	8
2	4	14
3	7	20
1	1	8
2	5	16
3	9	24

Page 58

[1] 16 with just the corners touching.   [2] 8   [3] 20 with just the corners touching.   [4] 10

Page 59

[3]

Number of triangles	Biggest perimeter (cm)	Smallest perimeter (cm)
1	3	3
2	6	4
3	9	5
4	12	6

[4]   24   72   14

Unit 7 Below zero

Activities

Materials required

Going below zero

 Thermometers
Newspapers
Travel brochures

Hot and cold around the world

  14–16
Counters
Paper clips

The lift game

  17, 18

🖥 Computing references

Links with National Curriculum Attainment Targets: Programmes of Study level descriptors

NAT	Level	PoS Descriptor(s)
2	3	i, k
3	3	b

Teaching suggestions

This unit introduces directed numbers by reading scales and games.

Going below zero

This activity is an introduction to numbers below zero designed to encourage accurate reading; and for experience of possible rounding up or down between temperature marks. It is important to watch that the thermometer is not held in the wrong place.

Hot and cold around the world

This is a game to familiarise pupils with the language which might be used when dealing with temperature changes. It will help them to be aware of the positions and moves on a thermometer. The game is designed for *two* or *three* players. Each player will need a paper clip, a temperature gauge and some counters.

Each player starts off at 0° and they take it in turns to lift one card and act on the instructions, e.g. 'Rise +5°'. When a player lands on a temperature which corresponds to the temperature assigned to a city, the player captures that city by putting a counter on it. Only one person can gain a particular city. The winner is the player who has the most cities.

This game will bring out a lot of conflict because pupils will have to consider whether the cards they have picked will allow them to move at all, as well as where they are moving to – e.g. if a player on 28 picks up 'Rise +5°', this is not possible so the move is forfeited.

The lift game

This is an extension activity on negative numbers. Pupils develop this by making up their own set of numbers.

At the dockside

This activity allows pupils to make up their own questions or statements from a visual context.

They can extend this by drawing their own context. Watch for correct labelling of the directed number line. This exercise is good for a wall display, including the questions made up by pupils for others to answer.

Answers

Page 64

1

Statement	True/False	Comment
1	True	
2	False	The swimmer is 4 m above the red fish.
3	False	The ladder is 8 m long.
4	False	The octopus is 1 m below the bottom of the boat.
5	True	